T0149590

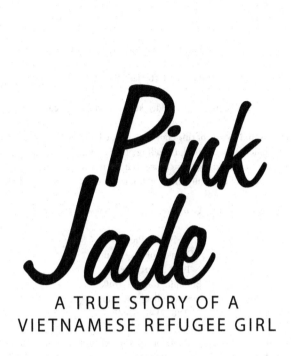

Pink Jade

A TRUE STORY OF A VIETNAMESE REFUGEE GIRL

Jade Balden

BALBOA.
PRESS

A DIVISION OF HAY HOUSE

Balboa Press books may be ordered through booksellers or by contacting:

Balboa Press
A Division of Hay House
1663 Liberty Drive
Bloomington, IN 47403
www.balboapress.com
1 (877) 407-4847

Because of the dynamic nature of the Internet, any web addresses or links contained in this book may have changed since publication and may no longer be valid. The views expressed in this work are solely those of the author and do not necessarily reflect the views of the publisher, and the publisher hereby disclaims any responsibility for them.

The author of this book does not dispense medical advice or prescribe the use of any technique as a form of treatment for physical, emotional, or medical problems without the advice of a physician, either directly or indirectly. The intent of the author is only to offer information of a general nature to help you in your quest for emotional and spiritual well-being. In the event you use any of the information in this book for yourself, which is your constitutional right, the author and the publisher assume no responsibility for your actions.

Any people depicted in stock imagery provided by Thinkstock are models, and such images are being used for illustrative purposes only.
Certain stock imagery © Thinkstock.

Print information available on the last page.

ISBN: 978-1-5043-9128-3 (sc)
ISBN: 978-1-5043-9130-6 (hc)
ISBN: 978-1-5043-9129-0 (e)

Library of Congress Control Number: 2017917276

Balboa Press rev. date: 11/15/2017

CONTENTS

I dedicate this book to all the Vietnamese people who escaped during this exodus and to refugees everywhere. May you heal and find peace and love.

1

Black Water

What is your favorite thing to play with? Take a look at your life right now. What does your world look like? Do you live in a home with painted walls, running water, electric lights, and convenient appliances?

We barely had electricity in our village. So naturally, there were no electronic toys like we have today! We didn't have carpet or tiled floors in our home. We didn't have running water. For a period, I didn't even have a dad.

I was born in a thatched hut in a war-torn country. The war had just ended, and everyone on each side had lost. The country was bleeding. People were hungry, desperate, lost, angry, vengeful, and confused. Death was a common visitor in our small village—and in any village, for that matter. People were fleeing the country in droves even though they had little chance of surviving the flight.

My family was caught in the middle of this. This is our story.

My name is Cẩm Hường, which means "pink jade" in Vietnamese. I was born in 1978—a few years after the Vietnam War officially ended. Our home was a small, thatched hut with dirt floors, and it was located in a village in the province of Cà Mau. Cà Mau means "black water" in the Khmer language.[1] The walls and roofs of the humble homes were made of thatch, a weaving of straw, palm leaves, reeds, or similar material. This seaside village was surrounded by water that was heavily mixed with dark-colored silt, which made the water dark. Our home was in the southernmost part of the village, which itself was located on the very southern tip of Vietnam, where the South China Sea meets the Gulf of Thailand.

When I was born, I was loved and surrounded by family. At two years old, I was wandering in and out of homes around the village. My parents lived with my grandma and grandpa Huỳnh, my dad's parents. My two uncles and four

---

[1] The name Cà Mau stems from the words *tuk khmau* in the Khmer language, meaning "black water." Some sources say it means "black land" too. See Wikipedia, s.v. "Cà Mau," accessed August 18, 2017, https://en.wikipedia.org/wiki/C%C3%A0_Mau.

aunties also lived with us in our little thatched hut. Our cousins and other relatives lived in similar huts nearby.

My parents taught me to address everyone I met as an aunt, uncle, or cousin, whether they were really related to me or not. In the small village, everyone knew my parents, and every adult in the village helped look after me and the other children. The adults kept an eye on the kids and reminded them to hurry home when it was mealtime.

My favorite person of all, however, was my dad. He was strong and hardworking, as well as quiet and often contemplative. Dad was slim, of medium height, and very gentle. At nineteen, he was already married to my mom. Their parents had arranged their marriage. I was born when he was only twenty. To me he was always loving, kind, and sincere.

Like all the poor villagers in the area, my family made a living by fishing. My dad went out to sea for several days at a time. Whenever he came home in his small boat, I looked forward to holding him tight and talking to him, telling him about everything that had happened at home and in the village while he was away. I followed him like a shadow and talked nonstop as he worked and listened. I was only two years old at the time. We were inseparable.

There was always something happening in the village. The dirt roads—everything was dirt, just dried-up dirt— were narrow. Just the narrow roads separated the homes. From the homes, the smell of prawns and dried fish filled the air. The air itself was humid and thick, like a hot kitchen where housewives cooked soup. The sounds of babbling housewives and playing children mixed with the scented air. Because the walls were just thatch, the sounds, scents, and energy traveled as freely from home to home as the pets and children did. Thus, every home was a part of the homes around it.

Every home had the same basic necessities. Each had a few large terra-cotta pots of water, which the women filled at the local water source using buckets. The women balanced these buckets on long bamboo sticks on their shoulders. As the woman carried their water and did their cooking, cleaning, and household chores, they seemed to be copying the village culture they had observed others engaging in. They even dressed the same. All the women in the village wore pointy straw hats when in the sun and simple outfits called *aó bà ba* made from lightweight fabric, usually featuring dark colors and black pants. The men wore shorts, and the children wore similar outfits. All day long, the village was filled with activity.

PICTURE: *Aó bà ba* or simple outfit
made from lightweight fabric.

In contrast to the vibrant day, the night brought thick darkness. As darkness fell, the families gathered to mend fishing nets, talk, and reminisce about the events of the day. For many families, lamps and candles provided the only light at night. These lights, however, also presented a danger in the thatch houses: fires could easily occur in any home.

When I was two weeks old, our family narrowly escaped from such a fire. It happened one night when my mom and auntie had been lying on a bed and talking late into the night with the lamp on. When she married, my mom had gone to live with the family of her husband, as was the custom. My aunties, my dad's sisters, and my grandma all helped raise me. In Vietnamese culture, we don't refer to our aunts and uncles by their given names. We call them Auntie Eight or Uncle Two, corresponding to the order of birth in their family. So there I was with my mom, Auntie Eight, and Auntie Seven in a bed together in the home of my grandma and grandpa Huỳnh. I was a fussy newborn that night, so they had stayed up later than normal to settle me. Exhausted from a long night, the women had then fallen asleep and neglected to turn the lamp off. The wind swept through the thatch house and tipped the oil lamp over, which started burning the mosquito net that protected us from mosquitoes as we slept.

For some reason, my grandma was awake in the middle of the night, and when she came in and saw the flames, she screamed. She pulled on the mosquito net to disconnect it from the walls. The burning fabric fell on us and burned us—especially my chest, my tummy, and my mom's leg. The scars from that incident are still on our bodies to this day. But Grandma Huỳnh saved our lives that night.

Life was very fragile in Vietnam at the time. War between the North and the South had led to the death and displacement of many families. Families moved from place to place to find safety and to start a new life, sometimes several times over. My grandpa Huỳnh—my dad's dad—and his family had just moved to the fishing village from a farming village only a few years earlier. My grandpa Mai—my mom's dad—and his family had moved to the village only a few years before my grandpa Huỳnh's family.

The war, the moving, the displacement, and the destruction were why people in the village, and in many parts of Vietnam, were poor and didn't get a good education during those years of conflict. They were just trying to survive, and not all were successful. As a result of this conflict, up to three million Vietnamese people died.

When the war ended in April 1975, South Vietnam, where our family lived, had fallen to North Vietnam. We had lost the war. My parents describe the time as one of panic and chaos. The money changed several times, with the old currency becoming worthless. The only reliable currency was gold. New harsh, strict policies were introduced to these simple village people. Suddenly, you couldn't trust anyone. Even children were taught to report their parents for saying things against the government. Political propaganda from the communist government of the newly "united" Vietnam began to seep into the South. North Vietnamese soldiers, government officers, and citizens began to move into the South.

To exact revenge, to remove threats and resistance, and to "reeducate" the supporters of the South Vietnamese cause, the new government began a reeducation program. Between 1 million and 2.5 million South Vietnamese were captured and forcibly moved to work camps, where about 165,000 died in the harsh conditions.[2] The "new economic zones" program followed the reeducation program. Under the banner of this new program, the Vietnamese government forcibly relocated families in South Vietnam to new, uninhabited areas to clear the way for the more than one million North Vietnamese who moved into the south and central regions.[3] Our family almost got caught up in this wave of relocations.

My parents tell me the story of my grandpa Huỳnh. One day after the fall of South Vietnam and a few years before I was born, a government truck came to the village. The government officer in the truck had a list of names of local villagers who would have the honor of helping rebuild a new Vietnam. This was presented as a

---

[2] Alan Rohn, "What Happened after the Vietnam War," last modified April 14, 2016, accessed August 18, 2017, http://thevietnamwar.info/what-happened-after-the-vietnam-war.
[3] Ibid.

privilege to help the country make progress. The villagers gathered around the truck to listen to the names on the list. In retrospect, we think this was a list of people who had supported the Americans and the South Vietnamese government during the war. My grandpa Huỳnh had received a gun from either the Americans or the South Vietnamese government.

When they called Grandpa Huỳnh's name, Huỳnh Van Ba (Huỳnh Brother Three), he couldn't respond for some reason. When telling us the story later, Grandpa Huỳnh said he didn't really know the reason he couldn't respond—it just didn't feel right. The officer pointed to him and asked him what his name was. Grandpa Huỳnh lied. He said his name was Huỳnh Van Hai (Huỳnh Brother Two). Grandpa Huỳnh was not a good liar and usually did not respond very quickly, but this time he responded very quickly with a lie. That lie perhaps saved his life. When the officer had finished calling names, and as the truck loaded with village men was about to leave, another villager protested that he had been overlooked. He asked if he could come. They let him hop on. It is our belief that everyone taken on the truck that day died or was killed because no one ever heard of them again after that day.

Even in the midst of war and the after-war chaos, life went on. Though my parents' marriage was prearranged by their parents, love was with them from the beginning. Proper girls and boys in a village did not date—they did not even talk to each other. They sort of just looked at each other every once in a while.

My mom thought my dad was handsome. My dad had heard that my mom was respectful and hardworking. In village life, parents and boys valued these traits more than good looks. Looks were just extra. Mom had two suitors by the time she was seventeen. Her parents turned down these suitors. My dad was next. His parents arranged, through a village matchmaker, a meeting with my mom's parents to discuss possible betrothal. In Vietnamese culture, this meeting is called *đi hỏi cưới* ("proposal ceremony"). During this formal meeting, the parents of the boy bring tea and a special cake to the parents of the girl. After my dad's parents spoke to my mom's parents, my mom's parents brought my mom out and consulted with her. Mom didn't object, which meant yes. A formal engagement ceremony was arranged.

After the formal engagement ceremony and prior to the actual wedding, my dad wanted to learn more about whom he would be marrying. One night he snuck over to my grandpa Mai's home and spoke a few words with my mom through a hole in the wall. Being young and shy, they didn't have much to say. Then it started to rain, and Grandpa Mai came out to check on the house. When he heard someone talking, he asked Mom whom she was talking to. Dad ran home.

My parents were married at the end of 1977.

A year later, I was born.

2

Where's Dad?

One evening when I was two years old and while my dad was away fishing, Mom packed up a few of our things and left the village without warning with my brother Khen (pronounced Ken), me, and Auntie Seven and Uncle Six (my dad's younger brother and sister). We traveled to a nearby coastal village called Bạc Liêu—about a half day's journey away. A day earlier, Mom had hugged family members and sobbed uncontrollably. The air was heavy with worry and secrecy. I didn't understand what was going on, but I felt scared. In my fear, I asked many questions—especially regarding the whereabouts of my dad. In a low tone, my mom answered my questions as simply as she could. We waited in Bạc Liêu at a friend's house for five days.

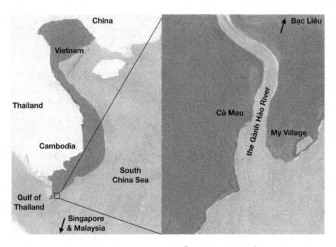

PICTURE: Map of Vietnam, the
surrounding regions, and my village.

Five days later, someone came to Mom and told her something troubling. Mom cried. We traveled home to our own village. Throughout the weeks that followed, whenever I asked anyone in our village about my father—"Do you know where my dad is, Auntie?" or "Uncle, do you know why my dad has been gone for so long?"—instead of receiving an answer, I would see sorry tears well up in people's eyes, and they would just hug and kiss me. I started to feel angry and frustrated.

Days and weeks passed. My mom was restless. I knew she was trying to stay strong for us, but I could tell she was terribly worried. After returning to Cà Mau, soldiers took her to their office a few times for questioning.

On some cold, windy days, she would wear my dad's

shirt and stand by the shore, staring out at the sea. Dad's shirt was a long-sleeved, cotton, button-down shirt with a collar. It was the type the men usually wore over the top of their clothes to keep warm. Because of the tropical climate in Vietnam, men usually wore tank tops if anything, and if they got cold, they wore long-sleeved shirts like Dad's shirt. One day when my mom wore it, I pulled at the shirt, shouted angrily at my mom, and made her take it off. "Give me back my dad's shirt!" I shouted as if it was her fault that Dad was gone. That made Mom cry. I cried too.

PICTURE: Crying with Mom while looking out to the sea.

I felt confused and helpless. What was happening? Where was my dad? Nothing was the same anymore. I would not understand the full story until many years later. No one spoke about it. The family kept everything secret.

I did not know at that time that my family had planned a secret escape from Vietnam, which had failed appallingly. Grandpa Huỳnh had sacrificed our fishing boat so that five of us (my dad, my uncle five, my mom, my brother, and I) could escape from Vietnam and from the new communist regime. This would allow for part of the family to go, and when they got to safety, they could help the rest of the family escape.

Our family needed help to survive and improve their situation. Life was difficult in Vietnam, and the family felt they didn't have a future if they stayed. It just wasn't safe anymore. Children couldn't even go to school and receive an education. Our family had heard rumors about people in wealthy countries, where they used gold to build the roads and where people could earn more money in one day than people in Vietnam could earn in a whole year. So sending some family members to a wealthy country seemed like it could help improve the whole family's welfare greatly.

In Vietnam, your family's welfare was the paramount concern in your life. People thought as a family, not as individuals. When they earned money, they earned money not for themselves but for the welfare of the family. They belonged to a group. Each member of the family had a role to play in improving the situation of the whole family. Everyone's actions and how each person performed his or her role would affect the rest of the family.

My mom, Mai Thị Nữa, described, in her own words, her role in the family's plan to escape:

My husband told me that the family had arranged for him, his brother, me, and our children to leave Vietnam on the family fishing boat. At the time, I didn't know any of the details of the plan. I understood only my part of the plan. The family was selling the family fishing boat to a man named Xia, whom I had never met. As part of the deal, my husband and Brother Five would captain the boat because the other passengers didn't have the skills needed. My husband would load the boat as if going out to sea to fish, so that the communist government would not suspect an escape. Then he would bring the boat in during the dark of night to pick up the remaining passengers and fresh supplies.

My part of the plan was to take the children to the markets in Bạc Liêu. Brother Six (twelve years old) and Sister Seven (ten years old) would accompany me. It was customary that if you went anywhere in the country in Vietnam, you always had someone go with you for protection. For Brother Six and Sister Seven, it was also a chance for them to go to the markets as well as help me with the children.

In our families, it was everyone's responsibility to help care for and raise the children. We didn't have a stroller like they do in Australia or America, so we had to carry baby Khen everywhere we went. He was only six months old at the time. Huong (Jade) was only two years old and could walk for herself, so she didn't need to be constantly carried. Moreover, Brother Six and Sister Seven also hoped to get on the boat and escape, if there was an opportunity to do so.

It would take about half a day to travel to the markets in Bạc Liêu. To get there, we would take a *ghe đò* (a ferryboat) for an hour and a half and then travel by *xe đò* (a coach or minibus). We stayed with mutual friends of Xia and Grandpa Huỳnh (my father-in-law). There we waited for someone to come and take us to shore to board the family fishing boat at night.

However, five days passed, and no one came. We didn't understand why it was taking so long. When someone did come, they brought startling news. They told us that the plan had been busted. The communist soldiers had intercepted some of the other passengers trying to leave. At that point, we didn't know where the boat was—whether it had been captured or whether it had gotten away. And

I didn't know if I would ever see my husband again. I had been able to say good-bye to him before he last left Cà Mau. However, I never intended that last good-bye to be permanent.

I cried all the way home to Cà Mau, where we retold the devastating news to the rest of the family.

The family was devastated. They had just lost the family fishing boat, their only source of income, and possibly the lives of two sons too. Grandpa Huỳnh had hoped to get enough money from the sale of the boat for the family to live on until he could arrange for the rest of the family to escape. The buyer of the fishing boat, however, never paid Grandpa Huỳnh, so poor Grandpa struggled to feed his large family without a boat for income—and without my dad and my uncle to help him work. For those who were left behind, life in Vietnam was tough—even tougher than before.

Our family wasn't any different from many other families in the area. Families suffered everywhere. Nothing was certain anymore. My grandpa Huỳnh and his family were just simple villagers trying to circumvent the invasive communist regime and improve the family's prospects in the face of a very scary and ever-changing world. It was frightening—especially as they witnessed daily the devastation and disaster in the lives of those around them. Death, dismemberment, disappearance, torture, imprisonment, and impoverishment were all normal parts of life now. So was hunger. That's why they had planned to escape.

Only later did it become clear to my mom what had happened to the family's plan. As part of the plan, by day the family fishing boat was to be anchored far out from shore, out to sea where communist soldiers could not see it. At night, it would come closer to shore. They would then take a little rowboat to shore and sneak one small group of five to ten people out to the fishing boat at a time.

It took much longer than expected to pick up passengers, however. Somehow (and we still don't know how) the plan was discovered, and our family was left without my dad, my uncle five, and the family fishing boat—all gone without a word.

Escaping was dangerous. Any people planning to escape kept their plans secret to protect themselves and their family. The communist regime severely punished people who were caught even planning to escape Vietnam. Death, imprisonment, or torture was the common treatment.

In the aftermath of the failed plan, the family was in a mess. The communists suspected them of having been involved in an escape or escape attempt. My mom was interrogated. They asked her where her husband was. My grandma and grandpa Huỳnh were also interrogated. The communists took them in for interrogation several times. They asked them where the fishing boat was and where their sons were, and Grandma and Grandpa simply told them they didn't know.

3

Left Behind

My mom, Mai Thị Nữa, described in her own words what followed:

We had to continue to live and to make do with what we had even though my husband wasn't coming back from fishing trips anymore. The future was unknown, and we didn't know what was going to happen. Here I was—I didn't have a husband, and I had two small children. People would see my situation, and they would talk behind my back. People felt sorry for me.

I felt incomplete. I couldn't go back to my family because I belonged to my husband's family; however, my husband was no longer there. Life was hard. The youngest of my new brothers and sisters were only slightly older than my own children. I was expected to work and to care for the others.

My mom had to adjust to life without my dad. She was a married woman without a husband—which was not a good status to have in a small village. She felt out of place and perhaps even like a burden to the family. Many people in the village took pity on her. She yearned to find a way to escape too.

At one point, a family in the village offered to let my mom join them in their escape. But she hesitated. What if her husband had survived? She needed to be around to receive the news. But if she didn't take this offer now, she might not have another chance. She hesitated for a time and finally refused. That family escaped without her. Not one member of that party was ever heard of again. Even after twelve years, when my mom returned to Vietnam and inquired about them, no one had ever heard of their whereabouts, not their family, their friends, or any neighbors in the village. We can only assume they didn't survive the escape, like many of the refugees at the time. If my mother had gone with them, she might have suffered the same fate.

Months went by, and still we received no news of Dad and Uncle Five. We all wondered whether they had survived and, if they had, whether they were safe and had managed to find refuge.

Death was common in Vietnam during that time. People died of starvation, died of persecution, died fighting for freedom, and even died of escaping. A large majority of these people escaped by boat, *vượt biển*. The United Nations High Commission for Refugees estimated that during this "exodus" of Vietnamese people escaping Vietnam, between 200,000 and 400,000 of these "boat people" died at sea from starvation, overcrowded boats, storms, disease, thirst, piracy, and boat failure.[4]

Every day, dead bodies of would-be escapees washed up on the shore. Every day, those who had been left behind, hoping for some news, any news, of their fleeing family members, went down to the beach to possibly identify the bodies of their loved ones. My mom couldn't bring herself to go down among them and search for Dad's body. She just waited for the news to come to her. She would stand at the edge of the sea with me and search the horizon for a sign of my dad returning as if from a routine fishing trip.

One day, to our great relief, my mom received a telegram from Singapore. He was alive. Dad had sent three short telegram messages from a Singapore refugee camp. One telegram was to my mom, the second to his

---

[4] See Wikipedia, s.v. "Vietnamese boat people," accessed August 24, 2017, https://en.wikipedia.org/wiki/Vietnamese_boat_people.

parents, and the third to my mom's parents. Dad sent three telegrams because he wasn't sure of everyone's situation back home, and he wanted to make sure his news got delivered. He told them that he and his brother were safe in a Singaporean refugee camp and were waiting to be sponsored to Australia. Our whole family cried with relief.

About three months after Dad's arrival in the Singaporean refugee camp, he was sponsored to Australia. After he reached Australia, to our delight a short handwritten note arrived. In a few poorly written words we learned that Dad and Uncle Five had successfully found refuge in Australia. The whole family gathered around to hear the short letter read out loud. We all hugged each other and again cried with relief. The letter was read and reread over and over. Our hearts filled with hope and joy again. We were glad they were safe and well.

Mom now had a new hope and purpose: she was determined to reunite with Dad. Whenever she heard a rumor of people planning an escape, she would secretly ask them to allow her to come along. She resorted to begging them to take us. However, no one wanted to take her—especially since she had two children to care for and couldn't pay for her passage. But she tried anyway.

4

What Happened to Dad?

My dad, Huỳnh Van Khanh, described his gratitude in his own words:

I would like to express a profound gratitude to anyone from America, Canada, the UK, or Australia who reads this story. I want you to know that I am grateful to you and that our happiness and peace is possible because of your generosity. Thank you for my life and for opening your hearts and your doors. For the past twenty years, I have been wanting to say thank you to the world for the chance at a better life. These are not just words; I feel it truly and deeply in my heart.

Specifically, I am grateful for the captain of the HMS *Texaco Bombay* and his wife—he was the captain of the ship that rescued us. I feel such profound gratitude even after these many years. I am grateful that you are about to hear my story.

Dad's boat was a little boat, about forty feet by ten feet (about twelve meters by three meters). Ultimately, it had become overcrowded with fifty-six people: fifty men, four women, and two children. They were unprepared for their journey into the unknown. They had little food among them, and their water supply had dwindled during their attempt to gather passengers.

On the day that Dad's fishing boat first left the village, it had been important that my father and uncle appear to the communist guards to be merely going on a routine fishing trip. Thus, they had to subtly return in the dark of night to pick up passengers and supplies for their escape journey. The fishing boat came close enough to shore to allow a small rowboat to go in for passengers and supplies while staying far enough away from shore to escape detection.

However, this process took longer than they had planned, and ultimately, they were not able to finish preparations and pickups. Dad's fishing boat had been out at sea for five days already. They still needed to pick up more supplies such as fresh water and more passengers, including me, Mom, and my brother, Khen. On the fifth night, however, somehow the communist soldiers discovered one of the groups escaping and started shooting randomly as the rowboat made its way out to the fishing boat. As this frightened group of people arrived to the fishing boat, they told the other boat passengers that everyone else had been captured and their plan had been discovered.

Panic gripped those fifty-six passengers. Gunshots came from the shore—a lot of gunshots. They could not return to shore without a risk of being captured and possibly never having this opportunity to escape again. Or they might never again see Vietnam, their homeland, or their families. It's likely that those fifty-six passengers imagined torture and government retribution, commonly rumored among their people at that time. They needed to decide and act quickly.

"We have to go now," the passengers shouted. "Otherwise we will die!" The passengers knew they didn't have enough food or water for their journey, but they had little choice. My dad, the captain, hesitated for other reasons: he had not picked up his wife, son, and daughter. The organizer of the escape pointed a gun at my dad and said something like "Get us out of here. We need to leave now." Dad started the boat's motor and turned the boat out toward the sea.

As he headed out to the open sea and as the view of Vietnam grew smaller and smaller, his heart sank and started to ache, and then he cried openly. As the panic of escaping the gunshots subsided, he began to process what was happening. He did not know what had happened to his wife and children who had been left behind, but he assumed we had been captured along with the other people. Would he and his brother ever see any member of their family again? Would they ever be able to return home to Vietnam again? Heartache consumed him.

My dad's life was now set on an entirely unexpected course. He was only about twenty-two years old at the time. For him, the way ahead was uncharted, unknown, and foreign. What would his life be like without everyone he had ever known? As he watched the sea open up to him, he wondered, where would he find refuge? What country would let him in? Would he even survive this voyage?

When I later asked my dad if he was scared we had been killed, he told me he had hoped we would not be killed. After some thought, he had reasoned that the communist preferred to capture escapees. They would take the escapees' money and throw them in jail for a few months. They would shoot at them only to scare them if they tried to run, so that they could capture them and take them to jail. So he wasn't afraid that we would be killed, but he suspected that we had been captured. As it turned out, we hadn't been.

How could the escape have gone so badly? These were uneducated villagers trying to organize something complex in secret without arising suspicion. They had not been allowed to gather in advance. They didn't understand everything that was happening. There had been no meeting to discuss it. They didn't have experience. They barely even trusted each other. Dad and Uncle Five were fishermen and knew how to navigate the sea. Xia, the boat buyer and escape organizer, was a city person and didn't know anything about the sea. He wanted as much money (in the form of gold) as he could get before they left. So he had arranged to keep going to shore to pick up more people and get more money. He had purposefully left Mom, Khen, and me for last, to maintain leverage over my dad. Xia understood that my dad would not leave without him when Xia went in to shore to pick up more people or supplies. So in the end, not only had we been left behind, but so had the supplies.

So there they were out at sea and unprepared. The five days of waiting and picking up passengers had depleted their food and water supplies. They would soon be hungry and thirsty. Hunger was a part of life that they had become accustomed to in Vietnam. But now, with nothing to do but wait, they had little else to think about, so it hurt more.

Dad and his fellow refugees traveled for days on the wide-open waters. There was nothing to see in any direction. Dad said he felt like a little ant on the seemingly infinite sea. He remembers the dolphins occasionally swimming alongside their boat. The dolphins became welcomed, curious, momentary distractions from the passengers' life-threatening distress. When these distractions swam away, they had to face the inevitable: starvation. They ran out of fresh water completely on the second day after their escape.

Hoping for some way to get more water, they scanned the horizon for fishing boats that they could barter with. They spotted a boat and began to move toward it. But what they thought was a Thai fishing boat turned out to be a Thai pirate boat. At that time in the Gulf of Thailand, numerous Vietnamese refugees escaping their homeland found themselves stranded at sea, disadvantaged and vulnerable. These simple people were escaping from their repressed lives in Vietnam and seeking freedom elsewhere. The escapees often carried gold because Vietnamese money at the time was worthless. The currency had changed four times already, and so it had little or no value, especially to people overseas. The escapees were also often defenseless, hungry, poor, and distressed. Thai seamen began to exploit their desperate situation. Some Thai seamen soon went to the extremes of robbing, beating, raping, and even killing their victims for sport. The stories are horrific.

One story of people we knew who encountered pirates

during their escape was particularly horrific. The pirates killed the men and children, sank the boat, and took the women to a remote island to be continually abused and assaulted by visiting pirates. Only one woman from that party survived to tell her story.

When Dad's boat pulled up to the Thai boat, they asked the Thai seamen for water. The Thai seamen entered my dad's boat and pulled out knives. These pirates wanted money. It was generally known that most of the escapees would have some gold on them to help start their lives in their new country. They generally sewed this gold into their clothes to keep it safe and secret. The theme of sewing gold and jewels into clothing runs among all the world's refugees. Think of the Jews of Germany, the Cambodians, the Russians or French aristocrats, and many others.

The parents of a Vietnamese friend with whom I would later grow up in Australia had hidden most of their entire family wealth in gold sewn into a thick belt attached to a pair of pants, which the mom wore. They had been a wealthy family in Vietnam and were hoping to take that wealth with them. They too encountered pirates and lost it all. They felt devastated. Many escapees, out of fear, would yield their treasures without much provocation, hoping to escape death, abuse, or bodily harm.

The pirates whom Dad and his fellow passengers

encountered demanded gold from everyone on the boat. Up until then, the passengers had been unaware of how much gold everyone was carrying; that was a private matter. As they pulled out their gold, it was discovered they all had about an ounce. My dad had only half an ounce, but after they were robbed, they were all equally poor. Thankfully, no one was hurt in the process.

There were four women on the boat, and it seemed the pirates were about to rape them. However, the pirates' captain interceded. Dad said that the captain was a nice Chinese man. For some reason, he forbade his crew from raping the women or otherwise harming the passengers on Dad's boat.

In an ironic twist of fortune, the pirates gave Dad's boat four baskets of ice, which fishermen typically kept on hand to keep their fish fresh. Dad's crew put the ice in a two-hundred-liter drum. They now had fresh water to drink. Their lives had been spared—at least for now. Now they had water, but their food supplies were running dangerously low.

5

Hope on the Horizon

The escapees on Dad's boat focused their efforts on being rescued. It was not clear where they were headed at that point. They did not have enough provisions to get to safety. They just hoped to be rescued at sea. All the people on the boat waved arms and flags at big cargo ships whenever they spotted them in the distance. However, these ships either didn't see them or chose to ignore them. In retrospect, my dad speculated that if they did see his boat and chose not to pick them up, it wasn't because they didn't have compassion. It would have been very difficult and costly, in terms of both time and money, to pick up refugees in the area. Moreover, the people on the ships were likely following orders from their employers and may not have had the authority to offer assistance even if they wanted to. So my dad didn't blame the passing ships.

Every time they saw a ship pass in the distance, their hopes were raised and then shattered when the ship disappeared again into the horizon. Three of these ships, either big cargo ships or oil tankers, came and went all around the same time, the day after the encounter with the pirates.

Dad's little boat had been out on the high sea for three days and three nights. Many of the passengers were not familiar with life at sea. Those who were unfamiliar were prone to become seasick, throw up, and feel dizzy to the point of incapacitation. Most of the inexperienced sea-travelers just lay there prostrate as the boat floated further into the ocean's wide, seemingly infinite expanse. For most of the time, there was nothing on the horizon—nothing for the eye to hold onto. Being so small and lost in something so big was very frightening—especially with their food supply running out.

Finally, the supplies completely ran out, and the people on the boat were consumed by both hunger and thirst. The passengers grew weaker. They had been skinny when they left Vietnam. Now they appeared bonier and sunken—especially surrounded by salty seawater. Their skin also darkened in the sun. Between the bright sun and the salty seawater that dried on their skin, they appeared dry, dark, and dehydrated.

A fourth ship suddenly appeared on the horizon.

The wife of its captain was exercising on deck when she spotted my dad's boat. Dad believes that it was the wife's compassion that persuaded the captain to stop to pick up the refugees.

PICTURE: The impressive HMS *Texaco Bombay* oil tanker rescuing Dad's crew from the water.

When the refugees reached the ship, the impressive HMS *Texaco Bombay* oil tanker towered over Dad's boat. The fishing boat was very small (only forty feet long or about twelve meters) compared to the HMS *Texaco Bombay*, which was approximately 153 meters long by 24 meters wide (about five hundred by eighty feet).[5]

---

[5] See "Texaco Bombay—IMO 5058284," Shipspotting.com, accessed August 24, 2017, http://www.shipspotting.com/gallery/photo.php?lid=1655832.

The oil tanker, which was from England, was empty, so it sat very tall on the water. Although it had been only three days and three nights since the escapees fled the gunshots of the communist soldiers, Dad and his boat had been out at sea for five days before that. They would have starved before reaching shore unless they were rescued.

A crewman on the large oil ship used a loudspeaker to ask if anyone on Dad's boat spoke English. The captain of the oil tanker wanted to talk to the fishing boat captain before deciding what to do. Fortunately, Dad's boat did have an English speaker on board, Chị Hoa, one of the four women on the boat. Chị Hoa had married an American and was escaping Vietnam to be reunited with her husband in America. She had brought the only children on board, two Vietnamese American children.

The crew on the oil tanker lowered a rope ladder for Chi Hoa and my dad to come aboard to negotiate. Because of their weakened state, my dad was concerned that Chị Hoa might have difficulty climbing the ladder, so he had her climb up first. As my dad climbed up after her, he noticed blood running down her legs. Only a few days before, she had asked him a few times for some rags, and she had sat in only one place during the entire journey. He realized only later that she had needed the rags because she was menstruating. How difficult the journey must have been for her.

When Dad and Chi Hoa finally climbed onto the deck of the oil tanker, the cargo captain immediately asked, "What help do you need?"

"I need everyone on my ship to be rescued and taken to shore," Dad replied with Chi Hoa's help.

The cargo captain replied that he would have to contact the English government to ask for permission, so he asked Dad to wait. He left to make his inquiry. Although the crew members were from India, the captain and his wife were English, so he would have to answer to the English government. Around fifteen minutes later, he came back with wonderful news: the English government had given them permission to rescue Dad and his passengers and take them to a Singaporean refugee camp.

After all the passengers were on board the ship, the shipmen gave them milk to drink. They must have appeared very frail and weak to the shipmen. My dad was only 110 pounds (50 kilograms) at the time. Everyone was weak and dazed by now, but some had the strength to take a few sips. They couldn't drink much milk either because they had not been used to drinking milk in Vietnam and could not easily stomach it. Because they had just left their homeland, they were about to encounter many foods they were not accustomed to. Some people were too weak to eat, so they just sat in shock and simply stared vaguely. The shipmen tried to serve cold ice cream after the milk. They didn't even have time to get utensils before all the refugees dug in with their bare hands. Everyone knew what ice cream was.

Perhaps the sailors thought that Dad and his fellow boat people looked too skinny, weak, and likely to drop dead at any moment. They seemed to be in a hurry to feed and revive them. Dad remembers that he couldn't eat much. The shipmen did their best to give aid to my dad and his company, and my dad was very grateful to them. The memory of this rescue is etched deeply in his mind.

When retelling the story, my dad said that he wanted nothing more than to write to the captain, his wife, and their crew to thank them for saving his life. He is so grateful that all fifty-six passengers on his boat were spared, and he owes the preserving of their lives to the goodness of those seamen. He wonders where they are now and whether they understand how much of an impact that little act of compassion had on him and his life. He will never forget that day in May 1981 when he and his fellow refugees narrowly escaped a watery death.

The HMS *Texaco Bombay* set its course for Singapore, where its crew would deliver the refugees into the hands of others.

6

A New Direction

The large oil ship arrived at the refugee camp in Singapore on May 21, 1981. The most dangerous part of the journey was now over. Years later, Dad would share with me a newspaper article he read in August 1986, when they closed down the refugee camp. The article said that for every three people who had escaped Vietnam by boat, one person died in the attempted journey. One out of three! This was such a startling statistic to him at the time. It reminded him how easily he and his fellow refugees could have died.

Those who survived to make it to a refugee camp then had to hope that another country would allow them live in its borders. They were now homeless and country-less travelers relying on the generosity of foreigners in far-off lands to sponsor them. The refugee camps were like no-man's lands, where refugees waited for their fate to be decided. Some would be stuck in refugee camps for more than a decade. There are many sad tales of forgotten refugees who spent years of their life in this limbo.

Dad was fortunate, however. Once he was safe in Singapore, he wrote three letters to his family in Vietnam: a letter to his parents, a letter to my mom, and a letter to my mom's parents. He told everyone that he was safe and described his current situation. He told us how he was living and how he felt. When he had more news, he sent a telegram home. His family received the telegram before they received the letters. When I later asked him if it had been risky to send notes and letters back to family in Vietnam, he said that his letters were simple and to the point and didn't seem to be intercepted by the Vietnamese officials. He never received a reply, yet he kept writing anyway, telling the family about his plans and about life in the refugee camp.

These camps were not the safest places to live, but the refugees did not have the freedom to leave. The only hope they had to get out and make a new life elsewhere was to secure a sponsor from a developed country.[6]

---

[6] "From refugee camps in Southeast Asia, the great majority of boat people were resettled in developed countries, more than one-half in the United States and most of the remainder in Australia, Canada, France, Germany, and the United Kingdom." See Wikipedia, s.v. "Vietnamese boat people," accessed August 24, 2017, https://en.wikipedia.org/wiki/Vietnamese_boat_people.

From the beginning, Dad had hoped to settle in Australia—at least he had a hopeful prospect there. A friend on Dad's boat named Chú Tỷ had an uncle, Ông Mẫn (full name: Hò Minh Sơn), who lived in Australia. Ông Mẫn promised to sponsor Dad and Uncle Five to Australia in exchange for their helping his nephew, Chú Tỷ, escape Vietnam. Dad and Uncle Five had helped Chú Tỷ get passage on the boat and helped him throughout the journey. When there was a complication with the paperwork, Chú Tỷ urged his uncle to simplify and speed the process by completing his sponsorship first and leaving Dad and Uncle Five in Singapore. But true to his word, Ông Mẫn and his wife, Vỏ Thị Cộm, sponsored my dad and Uncle Five to Australia. Altogether, they stayed at the Singapore refugee camp for only three months—very fortunate.

On July 18, 1981, my dad and his younger brother, Uncle Five, arrived in Australia. Ông Mẫn and his wife were graceful and kind hosts. On his first day in Australia, during dinnertime at his host's home, Dad stared at his big bowl of *thịt kho và trứng gà*, rice with warm pieces of stewed meat and boiled egg. He could eat only half his bowl. As he stared, he thought of his family in Vietnam. *They must still be hungry,* he thought. *This big bowl could have fed my whole family! Here I am enjoying it all on my own while my family suffers hunger each day in Vietnam.* He wished with all his heart that he could share that bowl of food with us all. He thought of us, his parents, his little brother, and his four little sisters. The culture from his childhood was a culture of sharing: if you have anything, you share it with your family. In other words, you never keep food to yourself.

PICTURE: A typical bowl of *thịt kho và trứng gà*: rice, stewed meat, and eggs.

That evening, he borrowed a pen and paper, and in his unpracticed fisherman's hand, he wrote another short letter to us. Because of the war, his education had been sporadic. The pen felt awkward in his hand, but he had to let his family know that he was safe and well. The family in Vietnam didn't have a telephone, so the only way to communicate was by letter or telegram.

Dad lived with his hosts in Punchbowl, New South Wales, Australia, for eight months. He was so happy in Australia that he wanted to cry. The people were very generous. From the time he was very young, no one had ever given him anything this special before. He had never received this kind of treatment in Vietnam. In Australia, he had plenty of food to eat and a place to sleep. The people in the hostel gave him clothes and a medical exam.

The generosity of the Australians was so complete and detailed that he was amazed. He would remember the kindness of places such as St. Vincent De Paul, which helped refugees make a new life in Australia. They gave him clothes and a black-and-white TV. They even gave cash to people who had families. Most of the clothes the refugees were given were old and used, but Dad and the other refugees didn't see the clothes they received as old; the clothes were good, and they were grateful. This kind of abundant charity was an entirely new concept for him. He wanted to do everything he could to pay it forward and share his good fortune with his loved ones in Vietnam.

7

My Journey with Mom and Khen

Soon after she heard the news of Dad's arrival in Australia, my mom became focused and determined to leave Vietnam and join him.

She felt that we had no future in Vietnam—poverty was prevalent, and the hope of freedom had fled with the Americans. With this laser focus, she kept her ears and eyes open for any possibilities of escape. I kept asking, "Mom are we going to look for Dad?" She always comforted me, saying, "Yes, we will find Dad."

Upon hearing rumors of some of the neighboring families' secret plans for escape, my mom approached them and asked for passage. She had asked a group for passage before, but that group had disappeared and never been heard of again. I mentioned this group in chapter 3. In her heart, she was grateful she hadn't gone with those people. Besides, at that time, she hadn't known where my dad was and wanted to be there in the event he returned. Now that she knew where he was, she was ready to escape.

One of the first families my mom approached to ask for passage was a group of close relatives. However, they said they could not take her—probably because she would be a burden to the group or could not pay.

Every day brought news of someone's tragic loss, whether it was the bodies of loved ones washing up on the beach or families disappearing without a trace. We felt that we were protected and preserved by some divine power. Even with all the scary news, Mom did not fear. She told me later that I didn't allow her to be scared. I kept reminding her of our goal: finding Dad. My ever-eager spirit about being reunited with Dad kept her going all that time. Years later, she said that at twenty-one years old, she should have been scared, but she felt as if she was under some sort of powerful spell. She felt no fear despite having every reason to be scared. My mom was committed to finding a way out of Vietnam.

One day, out of the blue, a villager we called Bà Dì Năm Sen took pity on us and offered us the opportunity to come along with her family for free. She was planning to escape soon. Sweet Auntie Nam Sen was fond of my mom and knew of my mom's desire to leave Vietnam and to be reunited with her husband. She wanted no repayment from us. Mom was touched by her kindness. Auntie Nam Sen had a few kids of her own who were a little younger than Mom. Now every year, when we look back, my mom mentions how very grateful she was for the opportunity to leave with Auntie Nam Sen.

My mother is also especially grateful to my auntie Mợ Tư, her sister-in-law. When Mom told her we were leaving, Auntie Mợ Tư helped Mom pack, prepare food, and so on. My mom's mom, Grandma Mai, later found out that Auntie Mợ Tư not only had known about my mom's plans and not stopped her, but also and worse yet had helped her. Grandma Mai scolded Auntie Mợ Tư for covering for my mom.

As Mom was preparing to leave this time, she couldn't find the heart to say good-bye to her dad again. She told her sisters to promise to tell her dad only after we left. After four days, Grandpa Mai, my mom's dad, realized that he had not seen us around the village. He sat down at the table and asked my aunts and uncles, "They've gone, haven't they?" No one met his eyes or dared to reply, but the tears in their eyes confirmed his suspicions. Grandpa Mai was heartbroken. Grandma Mai was inconsolable.

The night we left, my mom carried Khen in her arms through the dark, damp forest. A fellow traveler, a dark skinny man in his midtwenties, carried me. He had a pointy face and called himself Chú Hải. His name meant 'ocean, which was ironic because he would escape by boat, *vượt biển*, twice and yet never really escape. I'll share his story in a moment. This attempt to escape with us would be his first. He had left his family behind and traveled with us in silence.

A few other escapees followed us through the forest in the dark. We were walking to a small rowboat that would take us out to a fishing boat in the Gành Hào River. The party would need to travel through the jungle via a smaller canal to get to an outlet that was less heavily guarded. The route was as complicated as it was covert.

In the forest, we had to keep very quiet, so I tried not to talk, which was difficult for me. We did not want the communist soldiers to find out what we were doing. My baby brother Khen got scared and abruptly started crying. We all panicked. It was dark, and I could not see anyone's face. A lady behind us called out under her breath, "Kill him, kill him quickly. He will give us all away." Mom covered Khen's mouth and begged him to stop.

Anger and resentment boiled up inside of me. I stared in the direction of the mean woman. How could she say such a thing? Khen was only a baby! Notwithstanding my anger, I continued to be quiet and did as I was told. Khen finally settled down, and we continued in silence.

The rowboat took us all to the old fishing boat, and we quickly hid inside it. This fishing boat was thirty by forty feet (about nine by twelve meters) and now held twelve people. Everyone still had to keep quiet. There was a checkpoint where the river emptied into the South China Sea. Communist soldiers stationed there checked all fishing boats before they could leave the river and head out to sea. When we got to that checkpoint, I held my breath. After a little while, our boat was given permission to pass. The communist soldiers guarding the station didn't know we were underneath and hidden inside the boat. We heard the rumbling noise of another boat nearby, which had passed the checkpoint too.

All night and into the next day, we sat still and traveled southward. The soldiers could still come chasing after us in their boats if they suspected there were hidden people escaping in our boat. Late into the next day, our motor spluttered and then stopped. We were terrified. What should we do now? As we slowly emerged onto the small deck, we saw people on the other fishing boat that had passed the checkpoint at the same time. There were women and children on that boat as well. We looked at one another knowingly. Both our boats were escaping Vietnam. We both had gotten past the guards. Then we watched as they continued to move ahead, leaving us far behind as we drifted slowly, going nowhere.

PICTURE: We ran into other refugees fleeing from Vietnam.

In frustration, Auntie Nam Sen and her husband started to argue over whose fault it was that the motor had died. Chú Hải diligently worked on fixing the motor, ignoring the fight. For days, we sat motionless, drifting on the water. Some evenings, the rough storms threatened to tip our little fishing boat over. Auntie Nam Sen and her husband continued to argue on and off about who was to blame for the state of the motor.

Life on the boat was difficult. After a few days, our food supply had nearly run out. I had motion sickness and couldn't keep food down anyway. Soon after that, our water supply was gone too. It rained and stormed, sometimes all night and day. Water splashed into the boat. My mom held Khen most of the time. The boat tossed and drifted ever southward as we waited at the mercy of nature, wondering what our fate might be. Our little frightened group of refugees could do little to improve the situation except sit, wait, and conserve our strength.

Being a mother of young children during such an ordeal was distressing. Each day, my mom grew more distressed. A mother in a crisis situation needs to do the same things that mothers everywhere do: care for and feed her children and keep them clean. Staying clean was not a simple task for small children on a small boat. There was no toilet on the boat, so if you needed to relieve yourself, you simply did your business into the sea. During the long storms, she couldn't hold my brother over the edge of the boat for him to do his business, so she had to just let him do it on her. Yuck. The things mothers must do to survive and help their children survive. In any event, he wasn't eating much, so he didn't need to relieve himself much. He was uncomfortable and cried incessantly. I wanted to help my mother, but I was sick too, lying motionless on the floor of the boat. It was just difficult. None of us were eating much, except Khen, who was still nursing. This was just as well because there was nothing to eat.

Finally, however, my mother's breast milk dried up, and she didn't have any milk or anything else left to feed my brother. He cried a lot. Years later, as a mom myself, when I looked into my chubby six-month-old baby's eyes, that memory of my mom and baby brother came to me. I could not imagine the awful feeling of not being able to feed my child. My mom recalled thinking that if we drifted much longer, we all would surely die. Many years later, my mother still had nightmares about the pain of the experience and the fear of her child dying in her arms.

Most mothers would be racked with guilt in such a situation—telling themselves they should have prepared more or should have known better. However, as an uneducated, nearly illiterate twenty-one-year-old from a coastal village in a war-torn country, my mother had had no way of knowing what risk she was taking. She was very young and trying her best to survive in a difficult world. Life was so bad in Vietnam at the time that the thought of living in a free country had driven her to take this dramatic action. Many like her died in their attempt or suffered in greater ways than we did. However, I never heard my mother complain.

My mother has amazing strength of character. Every time she tells her escape story, she shares it in a matter-of-a-fact, undramatic way. It's only when retelling the story in English or thinking long about the story that I think, *Hold on, that was pretty scary.* She was always the strong one in her family. She had been the oldest sister in the family at home, which meant she'd had a lot of responsibilities. When she married my dad and went to live with his family, again she was the oldest girl at home and had many little siblings to take care of. Dad's two older sisters were married and had already left home. After Mom married into the family, whenever anyone at home was hungry or needed help, he or she would go find my mom. She has always been so selfless, almost to a fault.

This situation, however, stretched her to her limits. Sometimes when we hear stories such as this, we forget about the necessities of life that would exacerbate the plight of those experiencing a traumatic event, such as the need for fresh water, the lack of a place to go to the toilet, and the experience of dealing with issues such as menstruation, being ill with nothing to take for it, and body odor when people haven't bathed for several days and have lived crowded in a very confined space. Bad as these things were, they were the least of the worries. We were just focusing on staying alive. As each day passed, our boat drifted, and we felt like we were slowly dying.

PICTURE: This is roughly what that tiny boat looked like.

On the ninth day, Chú Hải had found a way to melt all the metal he could find and weld together some part the motor needed. The motor finally started spluttering and roaring back to life. We were moving forward again. Amazing. Now there was a glimmer of hope for us. Now we were ready to seek out salvation before we perished from lack of food and water. The Vietnamese term for escaping by sea is *vượt biển*, which literally means "overcome the ocean." It felt like the ocean had nearly overcome us. Although we were moving again, we still needed to either find shore or find someone to rescue us. As it turned out, we would find something just as good.

PICTURE: The oil rig rescuing us from the water.

Within a day or so of traveling on the open sea, we spotted a large oil rig in the distance. It seemed the wind and storms had taken us where we needed to go anyway. As we came closer to the structure, the workers on the oil rig waved their arms and shouted excitedly. We soon realized they were motioning for us to turn back around. As we looked behind us, we saw the very same boat that had left Vietnam at the same time we did. What a coincidence! But that wasn't the cause for alarm. A few of the men from that boat had hastily jumped into the water in an attempt to swim to the oil rig. It was then that we saw what the oil rig workers were shouting about: sharks. The water was infested with sharks, and the sharks were moving toward the men in the water.

For these men, this was a shocking end to a grueling journey. They had survived the dangers of the sea, and now they faced death on the doorstep of salvation. All efforts were focused on saving the men before they were devoured by sharks. In the end, we were able to save only one man. The other men perished in a cruel death, devoured by hungry sharks before our eyes.

Exhausted, hungry, and newly terrorized from watching these men die, the surviving passengers of these two little fishing boats, which had left the shores of Vietnam together, moved again toward the oil rig. The crew of the oil rig lowered a net for us. A few people at a time climbed into the net. I was too weak from hunger and seasickness, so I lay motionless as someone placed me into the net, which pulled us up to the platform.

PICTURE: Pulled to safety in a rescue net.

When all the people from both boats were on the oil rig platform, and before we could realize that we had actually survived, a hysterical woman from the other boat wailed loudly and ran straight toward my mom, shouting and screaming. She cried and repeatedly called out, "My son, my child, my son, my child!" She tugged on my fragile baby brother, yelling the whole time. My mom didn't know what was going on. She had just been saved, and now she was under attack and didn't understand why. My mom tried desperately to protect Khen from the hysterical woman's attack, pulling Khen's limp body back. I was scared because Khen was so small and so fragile. Others helped remove the woman and restrain her while we tried to understand what had just happened.

We soon learned why this woman was so beside herself. A few moments after she was restrained, she calmed down again. Her fellow boat passengers explained her situation and cause for hysteria. On the very same day our boat broke down and stopped working, their boat had gone straight into thieving Thai pirates. The pirates had robbed them, beaten their men, and intimately assaulted their women. The woman who was now so distraught had held onto her baby son, pleading with the pirates not to harm her. In response, two of the pirates had taken her baby, brutally killed him before her eyes, and then assaulted her. How horrible. How that poor woman must have felt.

We felt so sorry for the woman and for all the other passengers of that boat. At the same time, a wave of gratitude rushed over us as we realized we had been saved from that horrible pirate attack. Had our motor not broken down, we too might have met that tragic fate. Looking back, I know that for some reason, through divine intervention, our boat broke down at just the right time.

Now here we were: safe at last! We had overcome the sea. We had been saved from starvation, saved from pirates, saved from watery storms, and saved from the war-torn life of poverty in Vietnam that we were so desperate to leave behind. Now we would rely on the compassion of the oil rig workers to help us get to land.

8

Refugee Camps

The workers on the oil rig arranged for us to be sent to one of the refugee camps in Pulau Bidong, Malaysia. The camp was on a small island and covered the entire island, so there was no need for fences. These camps were crowded and dirty, and the air was humid and sticky. A feeling of confusion seemed to saturate the area. Needless to say, there was not much order.

Upon arriving at the camp, we entered the reception room to complete paperwork (nothing can save you from paperwork). Once new arrivals completed initial paperwork, they were offered a small bowl of instant noodles. My mom said it was so delicious that she had tears in her eyes. Khen and I couldn't eat it because we kept vomiting for days as a result of being dehydrated and undernourished. We were then taken to Zone A.

Zone A had tents made from branches and tarps—each about six square meters (approximately six feet by

nine feet) and housing about twelve refugees. Every time
it rained, coconuts would fall, and people occasionally got
hurt. Conditions were less than ideal, but we were grateful
to be alive and on solid ground.

One of the first things my mom did was send a letter
to Vietnam to let our remaining family know that we
were safe. She had to ask a literate person to write the
letter for her because she could not write. She also sent
letters to Dad in Australia.

Upon receiving our letter, in a flurry of joy, Dad
immediately sent letters and money to us. However, we did
not receive them. Every time Dad sent a letter, he put some
cash into it to help us buy food and clothing in the refugee
camp. Unfortunately, he didn't know that his letters were
never delivered and that the money was stolen.

Many people had assistance from their families who
were living overseas. After some time, Mom wondered why
Dad hadn't written back. She was confused and worried
and felt abandoned. Month after month passed, and we still
did not hear from Dad. Mom began to lose hope. When
others in the camp teased me that my father had forgotten
us and had remarried another, it made matters worse. Did
he still care? Was he working on sponsoring us? It had
taken Dad only a few months to be sponsored to Australia.
Mom, Khen, and I had waited for many months already

without any indication that we were going to get out of the prisonlike camp.

As we waited, Mom did all she could to provide for us. She found a small piece of earth in which to plant herbs to sell to other refugees. We hadn't brought anything with us. Others had belongings such as tools or fishing gear. Mom tried to buy fish from the fishermen, which she cleaned, prepared, and resold for a small profit. We were able to get by, but living under these circumstances was very precarious. Besides providing for us, my mom also needed to protect us. The camps were not safe.

Two months after our arrival, my mom applied to be transferred to Zone F, which she considered a safer zone, because she was afraid we might get hurt in Zone A. She was allowed to transfer to Zone F, H16, which was a house with a tin roof that housed sixteen people. The house was about eighteen feet by twelve feet (approximately six meters by four meters). We stayed there for six months.

The neighbors in H15 helped some Malaysians go net fishing, and the Malaysians paid them with fish. Cô Thừa, the wife of one of the fishermen, would sell the fish every morning. One afternoon after Cô Thừa awoke from an afternoon nap, she walked to a hill adjacent to Zone F to relieve herself in the forest. She never returned.

When her husband awoke, he couldn't find her, so he reported her disappearance to the Malaysian police. The police found her body. She had been robbed, violated, and murdered. She had been carrying about an ounce of gold and a watch. Her husband must have been devastated. From then on, he was always in a bitter mood.

These terrible things were a part of life, but life didn't stop because of them. The officials kept the crime quiet and buried her body. The husband continued to fish. My mom begged him to let her sell fish for him. At first, he rudely said, "You don't have the money to buy any fish off me."

My mom begged, "Please. Let me sell the fish for you and pay you for the fish after." He finally agreed. She sold four fish for one unit of Malaysian currency and paid him the same amount for five fish. Therefore, she profited by one fish for her efforts to clean, prepare, and sell his fish.

One night at about 1:00 a.m. when the fishermen returned from fishing, she came to collect the fish and saw that there was a two-pound (roughly one-kilogram) squid. She asked him, "Could I sell that for you too?"

He said, "The squid is too expensive for you. You can't afford it." Then after a pause, he asked her, "Do you think you would be able to sell it if I let you take it?"

"I can sell it," she replied.

He gave her the squid and warned her, "You're dead if you lose this!"

"Don't worry. I'll keep it safe." She believed she could get three to four times more profit from squid than she could from fish. When she went back to bed, she lit her lamp made from a plastic milk bottle filled with cooking oil and salt. She sat there trying to stay awake while watching the squid until daylight, when everyone else would wake up.

Toward the end of the night, she began to doze off. She suddenly jerked awake to see a rat the size of a small cat dragging the squid down its hole. She chased after the rat and tugged the squid back, but half of the head was gone. She was still able to sell the squid but without any profit for herself. When she told her story to the fisherman, he laughed at her and scolded her for being foolish. She cried and asked him for a discount, but he simply said no.

I tried to do my part to help the family too. When we collected our weekly food rations, I would save and share my small box of raisins with Khen. We didn't have candy, so the raisins were the next best thing. It wasn't easy sharing the raisins at times. The camp organizers gave us a few bags of dried ramen noodles, a little rice, cooking oil, and some eggs. We didn't have some of the simple foods we now enjoy every day in the developed world.

One time, I saw a Malaysian man eating a crispy apple. I asked my mom for an apple, but she said she didn't have the money for one. I told her I would get us some. I waited for that same Malaysian man to come past our camp again. Then I ran out to him and asked him in Vietnamese if he would please give me an apple. He apparently understood me because he gave me two apples. I ran back to the camp and told Mom that I had gotten an apple for me and an apple for Khen.

We slept in bunks in big, long, makeshift shelters. There were rows and rows of bunk beds. With our living quarters so crowded, loud, and uncomfortable, my brother cried a lot. My mom made Khen a hammock to settle him, and even then, he would have moments of nonstop crying. It sometimes became overwhelming for Mom. When she lost hope, I would comfort her. "Mom, we are going to Australia. We will see Dad again." I repeated those words over and over again.

PICTURE: Mom, Khen, and me living
together at the refugee camp.

Some people in the camp made things difficult for us
for their entertainment. An old man and his wife enjoyed
teasing me, often suggesting aloud that my mom should
marry one of the men who had a confirmed sponsorship
in America or England. This made me mad. They liked
making me cry and turn argumentative. In frustration, I
argued back, "You marry them yourself. Don't make my
mom marry them! We are going to Australia to be with my
dad!" They laughed at me when I shouted like that. I said
to my mother, "Mom, don't listen to that crazy old man and
woman. If you do, you'll never get to meet Dad." My mom
told me later that those people loved hearing me express
such loyalty to my dad, so that's why they kept teasing me.

I turned three years old in the camp. We still hadn't heard from Dad. Some men tried to be friends with Mom. After all, she was very young and beautiful. I was pleased when she turned them all down. Mom had started working young, so she was very strong physically. In a way, she felt mature beyond her twenty-two years. Years later, after I grew up, Mom said that she had been grateful for my constant reminders. Every chance I got, I told everyone we met at the camp that we were going to Australia to meet my dad.

In Australia, Dad was trying unsuccessfully to sponsor us. A few bits of information that we were giving in our paperwork didn't match the information he was giving. Two of the many things that were wrong were my brother's and my birth dates. In Vietnamese, when you are born, you are *một tuổi*, or one age. However, this is confusing when translated to English, so the records indicated we were one year older than we really were. The refugee officers recorded our ages that way, and the information stuck. Later in Australia, this served as a blessing: Khen and I were able to legally learn how to drive early!

Everything seemed confusing at the camps. I remember the story of Chú Hải, the man who carried me through the damp forest when we escaped Vietnam. After arriving in the refugee camp, he felt very homesick for Vietnam. He missed his wife, his children, and the home country he had left behind. Only a few months after arriving with us in the refugee camp, he stole a boat and returned to Vietnam. Normally, to prevent refugees from escaping, the refugee administrators destroyed the boats the refugees arrived on, but for some unknown reason, our boat had not yet been destroyed. The Malaysian officials didn't even know Chú Hải had left. Ironically, about three days after he left the camp, they announced over the camp speakers that he had been granted sponsorship to Australia.

He sailed back to Vietnam alone. It was dangerous to go back the way we had come, so it was miraculous that he returned home alive. At that time in Vietnam, any attempt to escape might be punished by death or imprisonment. Sure enough, when he returned, the Vietnamese government imprisoned him immediately. He was badly beaten and tortured. He later told us that they beat him so badly that he bled all over. As they were beating him, he felt wetness and looked down to find his clothes were soaked with his own blood. He was imprisoned for six long years.

Soon after his release, he escaped Vietnam again. This time he escaped with his wife, children, brothers, and sisters. When they all arrived at the very same refugee camp in Pulau Bidong, Malaysia, that he had left more than six years before, the camp was closing because it had been so long since the war ended and the camp was no longer accepting Vietnamese political refugees. However, his files were still at the camp, so the officials would allow him, his wife, and his children to continue to Australia. Unfortunately, however, the rest of his family were to be returned. So the authorities in Malaysia shipped his siblings back to Vietnam.

Many years later, in 1988, on one of my mom's visits to Vietnam, Chú Hải had just been released from prison. She said that he looked worn-down and skinnier and had the sickly appearance of someone who had aged many years in a prison cell.

9

Corduroy Pants

Exactly a year had passed since we were rescued, and several good things happened all at once. Grandma and Grandpa Huỳnh surprisingly arrived at our same refugee camp in Pulau Bidong, with my uncle and aunts too! Many months after we left, they had felt the need to leave Vietnam too.

The other good news was that a letter from Dad finally arrived! He had discovered that all his letters had been stolen because they contained money. This time he used a different shipping method. Mom felt a little happier and more hopeful. We wondered how much longer we would be apart. It seemed like we had been waiting forever. People came and went, and we were still there at the camp. We felt forgotten.

It was almost my fourth birthday when we heard the news that we were all set to go to Australia! It was exactly what we had been longing to hear. The camp authorities moved us to another camp in Malaysia at

Sungai Besi to prepare us for our departure to Australia. We parted again with Grandma and Grandpa Huỳnh and the other extended family members. They would stay in the first refugee camp while we would travel on to make a new life in Australia. We were confident that we would see each other again soon.

The camp at Sungai Besi was different. The buildings were more permanent, and instead of giving us raw food to cook ourselves, every day the camp authorities gave us food that had already been cooked. We collected this food in the morning. One day, because my mom needed to hold Khen, I volunteered to carry our rations. As I carried the rations along the road, however, I tripped and spilled all the food on the ground. My mom must have been under quite a bit of stress because she yelled at me, and for the first and last time in my life, she spanked me. I said, "I've lost all our food, Mommy." That day, we would go hungry. My mom stood there with Khen and me on that dirty road, looking at our spilled food. We sat there and hugged and cried.

Once in a while different charity organizations sent used clothing to the camp. People accepted whatever they were given. We were so grateful when we got some clothing. I wanted to look good when I greeted my dad. One day in the camp, I noticed that another little girl about my age had the most beautiful pair of red corduroy jeans. I asked my mom for a pair like them. As much as she wanted to give me a pair, sadly she couldn't. I begged so often that it made her cry. Right before we left, however, somehow from somewhere, I got a brown pair of corduroy jeans just my size! I was so happy!

To impress Dad, Mom used the funds he had sent to get our hair permed. I had typical Vietnamese hair, straight and black, and my mom thought I would look cuter with curly hair. But we weren't accustomed to managing curly hair, so my perm turned out to be more of a big Afro on my head for a few weeks!

Some friends in the camp owned a camera. We asked them to take a few photos of us. In the photo my mom is carrying my brother, and my mom's friend Tien (who later would marry Uncle Five) is carrying me.

PICTURE: Tien (now Auntie Five), me, Mom, and Khen in a rare picture from camp.

10

Together Again

Our family had very few possessions, so we boarded the plane with just the clothes we were wearing and no luggage. Khen cried the whole way from Kuala Lumpur to Sydney. I sat in my seat looking at the airplane food without eating because I had motion sickness. What a relief it was when we landed! The plane slowed and stopped. In my heart, I knew my dad was inside the airport waiting for us. From the moment we stepped off the plane, I eagerly looked about for him. Before Mom could finish talking to the customs officer, I had left her and run outside the arrival gate all by myself (in the direction everyone else was going). Even though my mom fearfully called after me, I didn't listen; I kept running toward the gate.

Right outside the gate stood my dad, even more handsome than before. Tears ran down his face as he ran toward me. I ran into his arms, and he held me tight. It was a moment I had rehearsed in my mind over and over. Mom ran out the gate to find me safe in Dad's arms. Dad hugged us all, and we all cried. We were together again, safe, and in Australia!

PICTURE: Here I am with my dad a few days
after we arrived in Sydney, still at the refugee hostel.
I'm wearing my brown corduroy jeans.

PICTURE: Our whole family together again in
Australia a short time after our arrival.

11

Australia

Australia was very different. We were strangers in a new land. This was the first time we had ever slept in soft beds with mattresses. There were several rooms in our house. Dad drove a car! Even though the car was old, we loved it. We even took pictures with it.

PICTURE: My brother Khen and I on our loved family car.

Dad had worked double shifts each day at the paper factory as he prepared for our arrival. For two years, Dad and his brother had worked and saved money, and they had finally moved into a place of their own in Lakemba, New South Wales. He said he rarely saw the light of day. He left before the sun rose and came home after dark. Charity organizations donated old furniture and clothing to us. We felt so rich! Every weekend our family would drive around the neighborhood, exploring new places and things. Some of those new things were as simple as new foods.

I started preschool there. My parents didn't know what kids took to school for their lunches. So they packed what they thought was a nice lunch. For a drink bottle, they found a baby's bottle with a teat at the store, which they filled with orange juice for me. When they picked me up from school, the teacher sternly told them that I was too old to be drinking out of a baby bottle! My parents were so embarrassed.

By the end of the year, we moved to a slightly bigger house in Yagoona in preparation for the arrival of my grandma and grandpa Huỳnh and other family. This new house was close to shops and some fast-food restaurants. One day, I got very sick and lost my appetite. I was small and scrawny as it was, and they couldn't let me get thinner.

Dad went across the road to the Yagoona McDonald's restaurant, the very first McDonald's in Australia, and bought me a treat. He thought, perhaps, that if the food was a treat, I would make an effort to eat. He gave me a Filet-O-Fish sandwich. I had never tasted something that different and delicious before! It was my introduction to fast food.

Since officially I was one year older than I really was, I started kindergarten early. My parents enrolled me in Yagoona Public School. I was so small that the staff had a hard time finding a Yagoona Public School uniform small enough to fit me. Compared to the Australian kids, I looked so tiny. At one point, Dad took Khen and me to a doctor to make sure we were growing normally because we were just so little next to the big Aussie kids. My parents were eager to know what to do to help me fit in at school. The school staff gave them instructions for what to do through the help of an interpreter. My parents remembered the part about packing a lunch and a drink for me.

Another day, a helpful person told my parents about school photo day. My parents had had very little schooling during the war. They had never had photo day in Vietnam and didn't know what to expect. They were so excited because we owned very few photos. This was a big day! The weekend before photo day, we went to the markets and bought a beautiful pre-owned red velvet dress for me. On the morning of photo day, my dad did my hair. He had no idea how girls wore their hair, so he combed my hair to the side just like his hair. I excitedly wore my red velvet dress to school.

When I got to school, I discovered that everyone else was in his or her clean and ironed blue school uniform. Not only was I the only one out of uniform, but I also was in red! I felt so out of place! The photographer must have been perplexed but kindly allowed me to be in the photo and had me stand on the outside edge of the class. I still laugh when looking at that photo now. It was a good thing I was tiny and sort of hidden. Can you spot where I am?

PICTURE: My Yagoona Public School picture.

By the end of that year, my extended family had all arrived safely in Australia. Grandma and Grandpa Huỳnh and their children, my aunts and uncle, all arrived safely. We were all living in the same home again! My mom had also given birth to my sister, Jamie, by then. The house was getting very crowded.

Most people in Australia didn't have several families living together in the same house, so my parents moved out. Our little family moved to Wollongong, a two-hour drive south of Sydney. We rented a little unit on top of an old barbershop. To save money, Mom and Dad grew vegetables in the garden and fished at the local ports and wharfs. They compared everything they bought to the prices of things in Vietnam, so it was difficult to justify any unnecessary expenses. To earn money, they sewed clothes on an old sewing machine and an old overlocker (serger).

In the evenings, they went to English classes. For outings, we drove around town, looking at different sights. As a treat, once in a while Dad bought a single can of Coke, a pack of salt and vinegar chips, and a Picnic chocolate bar. All five of us shared these things with relish! We each took a small bite and giggled happily.

I couldn't speak English well enough yet. I was shy, and sometimes the other kids teased me. The kids pointed out the oriental shape of my eyes, the flattish shape of my nose, and everything else that was physically different about me. At times, I wondered what else was wrong with me. Why were they teasing me? I wanted to belong here too.

Whenever the ESL (English as a second language) teacher came to take me out of regular class, I felt keenly different from other kids. I was embarrassed to be me. How I longed to be blonde and blue-eyed. Even after a year of eating as much as I could, I continued to be the smallest kid in my class. I was reminded of my relative size on each school photo day when the teacher lined the kids up from shortest to tallest. On the first day of first grade (year one) at Port Kembla Public School, my new teacher thought I was so cute. She picked me up like a doll, took me over to a fellow teacher, and presented her new student to her friend. They pretended to play tug-of-war with me, each trying to claim me as her own.

My parents valued education and wanted me to have the education that they wished they had had. I tried my best in school. When the teacher told us that we would start learning our times tables, I went home and told my dad. He taught me how he had learned all the times tables by memorizing them through song, so I did the same and taught myself up to the twelve times tables by the end of first grade.

When I was about seven, I started having very scary, vivid nightmares. The traumas that our family had endured were catching up with me. My mind was trying to process and understand what had happened. I saw images of the sea, of the camp, and of death. These nightmares happened frequently. When I woke, it was still dark, my skin was sweaty, and my heart raced quickly. At first, I would just lie under the covers and wait for the scary images to go away.

One night, I couldn't sleep, and the house was quiet. I saw a man standing at the foot of my bed. "Dad?" I asked. "Dad?" I repeated. The man just stood there. One more time, I called out, "Dad!" My dad came in from the other room and walked right through the man. I held tightly onto my father and told him I had seen someone in my room. I asked my dad all sorts of questions about life, death, and the purpose of life. Now, as an adult, I recognize that I was suffering symptoms of posttraumatic stress disorder. Once the nightmares started, I had a hard time relaxing and having fun.

I had very few toys and even fewer friends. Charities and a few kind people had given us the secondhand toys we owned. I remember owning four Barbie dolls. I spent hours playing with them. Whenever I could, I made them clothes with fabric scraps and made furniture with cardboard. This was a pleasant change from the difficulties and stresses of school. When I was about eight years old, I made a friend who lived nearby. I was eager to share my treasured Barbie dolls with her, so I walked over to her house and shared them with her.

Our life had never been more peaceful, but my parents missed the rest of the family who were still living in Vietnam. They started sending money back to Vietnam to help relatives who had troubles.

One day, Mom and Dad excitedly told us to pack up because we were moving back to Sydney. They had saved enough money to buy a small home. Halfway to Sydney, my heart sank as I realized I had left my four Barbie dolls at my friend's house. I didn't want my parents to worry, so I kept it to myself. Years later, after I had four daughters, I told them that God had replaced my four dolls with four real dolls: them! I have been able to make costumes for them and have thoroughly enjoyed playing with my four real dolls!

PICTURE: My daughters wearing dresses I made for them.

PICTURE: My daughters wearing Halloween costumes
I sewed for them (Goldilocks and the Three Bears).

12

Growing Up

We soon moved to Birrong, a Sydney suburb near Yagoona, where we had lived when we first arrived in Australia. Mom and Dad bought a three-bedroom, fibro house that felt like a mansion to them. They were so happy; they stayed up all night wiping the floors and walls until they were all clean. This house was ours, and we loved it. Mom continued to sew clothes, and eventually Dad started working as a tiler. To save money, Mom sewed all my school uniforms, we fished on weekends, and we grew our own herbs and vegetables.

We continued exploring Australia every weekend. Our radius of exploration grew wider and wider. The outings felt like school excursions for all of us. We tried new foods and went to new places. Our family was so grateful to be safe and free. *We have so many things!* we thought. When we purchased a pre-owned piece of furniture, Dad would tell my siblings and me stories of how life in Vietnam had been for them and how this "new" piece of furniture was a luxury.

My parents regularly sent money to Vietnam to assist family members who were still living there and who were less fortunate than we were. Dad reminded me that we needed to give back because we have been given so much. He taught me to be grateful to the leaders of the world such as Malcolm Fraser, Margaret Thatcher, and Ronald Reagan. I heard these names repeated for years. He showed me pictures of them in the Vietnamese newspapers he would read.

School got a little easier after a while. After two years, I stopped going to ESL classes. By the time I was in the sixth grade (year six), I was able to read chapter books in English. For one assignment, the teacher asked us to write about a historical figure. The librarian suggested books about presidents and prime ministers. I picked the first president of America, George Washington, and selected a book on him.

The hardcover book was thick and had over two hundred pages! I had never read so many difficult words. I didn't understand how to skim for key words or summarize key points. I didn't know that I didn't need to read the whole book either. So I spent most of my days, nights, and weekends reading. I thought the other students must be much smarter than I was because they didn't seem worried about this assignment. I filled two A3 project books (notebooks), both sides of each page, with small, handwritten words and pictures. I wrote about George Washington's entire life from his birth to his death. In the corner of the last page of my assignment, I wrote a little note to the teacher: "Dear Mrs. Pacey, sorry my handwriting got messy. My hand got tired."

When Mrs. Pacey returned the marked reports to the class, I saw that the other children's assignments were no more than two project-book pages long. Mine was about twenty pages! That day, Mrs. Pacey called me up to the front of the class. I was always nervous when this happened. She held up my assignment, flipped through the pages, and showed it to the class. The other kids wore looks of surprise and amazement. I wasn't sure if I should be embarrassed or proud. The students applauded, and the teacher told me to see her at lunchtime. During lunch, she taught me how to summarize a whole paragraph into one sentence. Mrs. Pacey's love and attention to me gave me confidence. I felt that I could master the English language with hard work.

PICTURE: When I was in the sixth grade, I did
my own hair! I will never have bangs again.

School was easier after that. I continued to work hard
and helped my family in the evenings. I spoke English for
my parents and helped them fill out forms and documents.
When a big tree needed to be chopped down, I wrote a
letter to the local government council for my parents. I
tried to help out in other ways too. After school, I helped
Mom with her sewing, doing little easy jobs such as cutting
the loose threads or sewing on labels. At times, Mom and
Dad would stay up past midnight sewing. They wore out
their bodies and sacrificed so much.

There were days when I still felt conscious of how
different we were. Other kids had interesting, fun toys
and nice clothes. However, I saw how hard my parents

worked, so I couldn't find it in my heart to ask for things. My parents freely gave all they could to us if we ever needed or asked for anything. There was no need for a special occasion for them to give small gifts and clothing. My parents said yes more than they said no, so I didn't want to add to their burden by asking for things my friends had.

Mom worked from home so that we would always have a mother at home and good meals. Within five years, my parents paid off their thirty-year house mortgage. They felt so pleased, relieved, and free again. It was just as well that they were relieved of this burden because it was time to make a trip back to Vietnam.

It was around this time that the communist government changed its label for refugees from "traitors" to "Viet home-comers," or *Việt Kiều*. It was now safe to return to Vietnam to visit. The US trade embargo created in 1975 had denied Vietnam the right to trade with other non-communist countries such as the United States and Australia. Vietnam had become increasingly poor during those years. It would not be until 1994 that President Bill Clinton would lift this trade embargo completely. Vietnam was closed off from business relations with the United States for nineteen years. Vietnam desperately needed money coming in from "Viet home-comers."

Within a year, my parents saved enough money to take us all back to Vietnam to visit family. They had longed for and anticipated this opportunity for almost eight years. I no longer remembered what Vietnam was like.

We packed old clothing and lots of cash to give away. In 1989, when we arrived, Vietnam looked and smelled like a bowl of Vietnamese *phở* noodle soup! The air was warm, humid, and mixed with spices and smells. People were everywhere, busily moving about in all directions at the markets, on the streets, and even in their homes. Usually, each home was small and shared by several related families.

My dad eagerly spent time teaching me and my siblings the Vietnamese culture. He showed us where rice came from and taught us the names of all sorts of interesting plants and fruits. For example, Vietnamese oranges are green; dragon fruits are pink and spiky with white flesh on the inside; durian fruit looks scary but tastes like sweet, buttery cream; and mangosteen fruit looks ordinary on the outside, but when cut open, it reveals an amazing lemonade-flavored fruit on the inside.

We made our way down to the village where I had been born. The small thatched-roof hut I was born in now was long gone. So were half of the homes around it. Time, wind, and water had eroded them away—one of the realities of living on a delta. I was reintroduced to my relatives and to half the village. They were all eager to meet us.

One wonderful experience was meeting up with Chú Hải again. I remembered him as the man who had carried me when we escaped and who had fixed the motor on our boat when it was broken. He told us his story (the one I shared earlier about him stealing a boat to return to Vietnam). During all this time that our family had enjoyed peace and comfort in Australia, he had been in prison in South Vietnam. He only recently had been released from prison when we met him. My dad pointed out that Chú Hải's daughter was my age. She was living in the village and didn't have the blessings of the education and freedom that I had in Australia. A sense of reverence and clarity came over me. How miraculous was my life's journey?

We gave a lot of money and gifts to people in Vietnam. There were so many wounded adults and disabled children begging on the streets. Many of them had missing limbs or other ailments. My siblings and I didn't know how to respond at first. We asked my parents what had happened to these people. Sometimes it was scary when we gave to one beggar and others would quickly throng us, making it hard to move. Sometimes they covered our taxi van window with their hands. They knocked on the windows.

I sometimes cracked the window open wide enough to push through a small bill for them.

What a state Vietnam was in! I wished I could help somehow. How could I give back?

13

Giving Back

My dad loves learning, and he continued to educate himself as he settled in Australia. I loved when he read the Vietnamese newspaper to me. He taught me all the things he learned. Dad told me about the world, the government leaders, and even funny stories he found in the paper.

Little did I understand then that this was one of the best ways for me to learn more about the world. My dad taught me to love books. One year, he took us kids to the Royal Easter Show (a big annual fair in the Sydney area). It was such an exciting treat. He stopped at the Britannica encyclopedia stall, and after pondering a moment, he asked me if these books would help me get a better education. I told him yes, not knowing at the time how much the set cost. With their minimum wage, it would take my parents several years to pay it off. Regardless of the sacrifice, my parents invested in a brand-new set of *World Book* encyclopedias and a set of *Childcraft* encyclopedias for our home. Dad and I would often sit and read these books as best we could and decipher them. Education was very important to my parents and was the one thing they were always willing to invest heavily in.

When I entered high school, I wanted to do well and was determined to make my parents proud. High school wasn't as hard as I had expected. My dad's efforts to teach me all he knew paid off. When we learned about the different countries and geography, it was easy for me because I had already visited those countries with my dad in our books. He had taught me about those faraway places so that I could have a better and more grateful perspective in my life.

During high school, which starts in the seventh grade in Australia, I tried to give back in different ways by volunteering and helping with organizations such as the Salvation Army Red Shield Appeal and by participating in other school-based charities. Giving back and finding purpose for my life helped alleviate the nightmares I was still experiencing.

In Australia, at the end of the school year, schools customarily hold a presentation day to award and recognize outstanding students. My parents faithfully came every year even though they couldn't understand most of what was said. This year I sat there wondering whether I would get an award. Wouldn't they be so proud of me? Then I heard my name called. I timidly walked to the stage. For my seventh-grade class, I was first in mathematics, first in English, first in history, first in geography, first in science, and first in health! I was first in all the subjects but one: PE, physical education. I was fourth in PE, and being one of the smallest and weakest kids, I couldn't have been more pleased with fourth place! I stood on the stage, receiving one award after another in shock. My parents looked on, clapped excitedly, and smiled. They were so proud. At the end of that year, the principal arranged an IQ test for me. Apparently, I did well because they assigned me to the selective class (a class for more advanced students), and I stayed in that class for the subsequent years of school. I realized then that there wasn't anything wrong with me after all. I was equal to anyone else in the world.

14

Full Circle

I graduated high school and went on to study law and international studies at Western Sydney University. Halfway through my first year, I had a change of heart and applied to a large private university in America. I wanted to study elementary education because I loved teaching, and I loved children. I really desired to give back in a way that would be meaningful to me. I felt that somehow I could find a way to help children all over the world receive a chance for a good education too.

And if I could one day go back to Vietnam, I could help children there and give them the privilege and opportunity I'd had, giving them a chance to change their life. I was thrilled when I was accepted to that private university in the United States. I attended Brigham Young University and did very well. The very last class I needed to take was Advanced English. I still felt nervous about English even after so many years, so I had saved this class for last. I was in the class with American students who had spoken English all their lives. Did I have it in me to do well in this class now? I did. At the end of the semester, I was one of the only two people in the class to receive an A grade!

While attending university, I had met and married my wonderful husband, an American. We soon had a beautiful daughter. Both my husband and I attended the same university. After I completed my student-teaching experience and my university requirements, I graduated with a bachelor of arts, majoring in elementary education.

My parents flew to America to be with me on my graduation day. They couldn't have been prouder. My dad had dreamed of seeing one of his children graduate from university. While sitting in the large arena, Dad looked down at me walking onto the stage and thought he saw the little girl who had been born in a thatched-roof hut in Vietnam once upon a time. He wondered at all the miracles that had led our family to this stage. His daughter was graduating from a popular American university just like other privileged kids.

Following graduation, we moved to Australia, where my husband could pursue a career in international business. We had three other beautiful daughters while living in Australia (that's four daughters altogether). A few years later, when my children had grown a bit, I decided to go back to teaching school. After I went through a short training to convert my US education to Australian standards, I was assigned to teach at Yagoona Public School! What a coincidence! I would return as a teacher to the same school where I had started kindergarten many years ago. I was excited.

Class 2B – 2013

PICTURE: Back at Yagoona Public School, this time as a teacher. This is the same school I attended as a small refugee girl. Again, I'm dressed differently than the others. Can you spot me?

On my first day as a teacher at Yagoona Public School, I stood at the gate for a moment. In my mind's eye, I saw a little me in a blue uniform dress running around on the grass, making daisy chains, and not understanding a bit of English. Now here I was in 2008, returning again to Yagoona Public School as a teacher.

In one of my classes, I taught a little boy who had just come from a refugee camp in Sierra Leone. I looked at that boy and had so much love for him. This was his first year in school, his first experience with formal education, and I was his teacher. I had come full circle.

I am grateful for the wonderful life I've been given, and I hope to continue giving back to a world that has taken such good care of me. I was a schoolteacher for eleven years and continued to serve people in different ways. I have now retired from teaching school and have created a business educating people about health and wellness using remedies such as essential oils and energy healing. At the time of this writing, I live in Florida with my husband and four daughters, and I enjoy every day of my life. If you would like to connect with me, please reach out to me at jadebalden.com.

My wish is to bring more peace to the world by helping people who also have suffered traumas in their lives—like I suffered. I want to help people learn to self-heal, become empowered, and give back. I also enjoy participating in humanitarian work that involves building schools in third-world countries, educating women, and bringing relief to other refugees. The world is such an amazing, abundant place, and we have so much to share.

As I have shared this story with others, I have observed how just hearing a story like this can inspire people. This was the driving force behind my desire to share my story with the world. I hope that in reading this story, you have felt inspired and uplifted. Thank you for joining me on this journey. May God bless you.

PICTURE: My family today.

Printed in the United States
By Bookmasters